Map My State

by Jennifer Boothroyd

Lerner Publications Company · Minneapolis

LERNER

SOURCE

Expand learning beyond the printed book. Download free, complementary educational resources for this book from our website, www.lerneresource.com.

The images in this book are used with the permission of: © Cusp/SuperStock, p. 4; © iStockphoto .com/crossroadscreative, p. 5; © iStockphoto.com/seamartini, p. 6; © iStockphoto.com/DNY59, pp. 7, 16; © iStockphoto.com/Shawn Gearhart, p. 8; © Laura Westlund/Independent Picture Service, pp. 9, 11, 12, 13, 14, 15, 17, 18, 19; © iStockphoto.com/Günay Mutlu, p. 10; © Todd Strand/Independent Picture Service, p. 21.

Front Cover: © Laura Westlund/Independent Picture Service.

Main body text set in ITC Avant Garde Gothic Std Medium 21/25.
Typeface provided by Adobe Systems.

Lerner Publications Company
A division of Lerner Publishing Group, Inc.
241 First Avenue North
Minneapolis, MN 55401 U.S.A.

Website address: www.lernerbooks.com

Library of Congress Cataloging-in-Publication Data

Boothroyd, Jennifer, 1972–
    Map my state / by Jennifer Boothroyd.
        p.   cm. — (First step nonfiction—Map it out)
    Includes index.
    ISBN 978–1–4677–1112–8 (lib. bdg. : alk. paper)
    ISBN 978–1–4677–1742–7 (eBook)
    1. Maps—Juvenile literature. I. Title.
GA105.6.B68 2014
526—dc23   2012045590

Manufactured in the United States of America
1 – PP – 7/15/13

Table of Contents

My family is planning a trip to Texas.

This **road map** shows many places in the state.

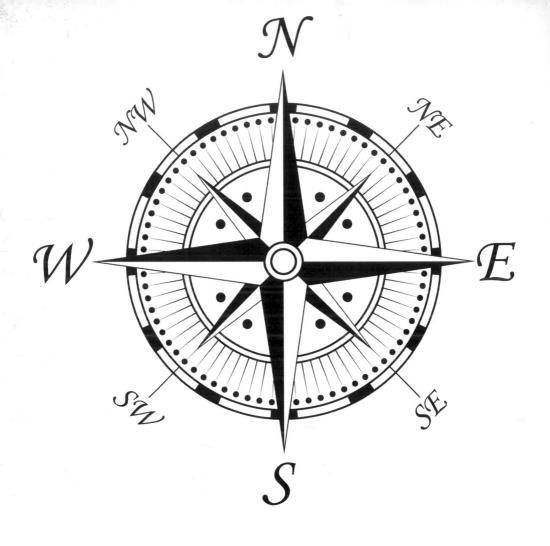

There is a **compass rose** on the map.

It shows the four **directions**.
The directions are north,
south, east, and west.   7

I will make a map. It will show the places I want to

8 see.

Route 66
The Alamo
Johnson Space Center
Austin
Guadalupe Peak
Big Bend National Park
Dallas
Rio Grande

This is a list of the places I chose.

A map has **symbols**. They stand for places.

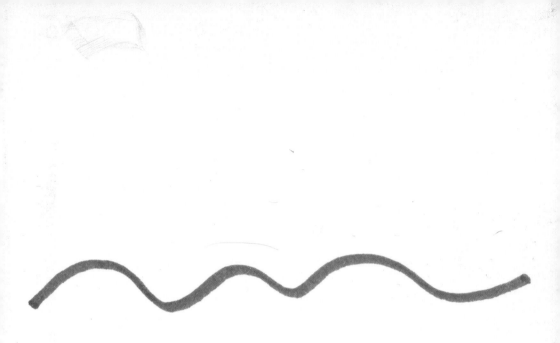

A blue line is a good
symbol for a river.

11

A brown triangle is a good
symbol for a mountain.

A star will be my symbol
for the **capital**.

I will make a **key**. It tells
what my symbols mean.

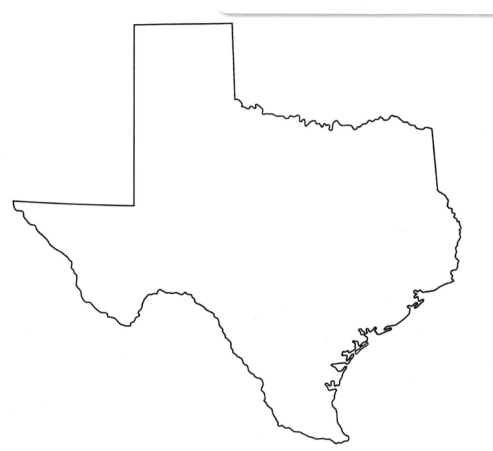

I printed a map of Texas.
It is blank.

I will use a road map to find the places I want to label.

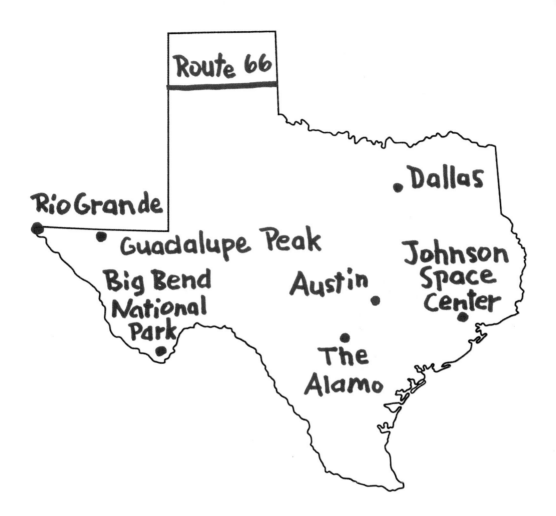

I labeled each place.

I added my symbols.

My map is done. I am
ready for my trip.

How to Make a State Map

1. Ask an adult to print out a blank map of your state.
2. Make a list of important places in your state.
3. Use a map to learn where the places are located.
4. Label each place.
5. Draw a symbol for each place.
6. Make a key to explain the symbols.

Fun Facts

- Texas is the second-largest state in the United States.

- Texas became a state in 1845.

- The Rio Grande is the longest river in Texas.

- Texas's nickname is the Lone Star State.

- Cowboy boots are the official footwear of Texas.

Glossary

capital – the place where a government is based

compass rose – a symbol that shows directions on a map

directions – one of four main points of a compass. The four directions are north, south, east, and west.

key – the part of a map that explains the symbols

road map – a drawing that shows where places and roads are

symbols – things that stand for something else

Index